First World War
and Army of Occupation
War Diary
France, Belgium and Germany

57 DIVISION
171 Infantry Brigade,
Brigade Machine Gun Company
10 February 1917 - 23 February 1918

WO95/2983/8

Published by

The Naval & Military Press Ltd

Unit 10 Ridgewood Industrial Park,

Uckfield, East Sussex,

TN22 5QE England

Tel: +44 (0) 1825 749494

www.naval-military-press.com

www.nmarchive.com

This diary has been reprinted in facsimile from the original. Any imperfections are inevitably reproduced and the quality may fall short of modern type and cartographic standards.

© **Crown Copyright**
Images reproduced by permission of The National Archives, London, England, 2015.

Contents

Document type	Place/Title	Date From	Date To
Heading	WO95/2983/8 57 Div 171 Infantry De Brigade Machine Gun Corps		
Heading	57th Division 171st Infy Bde 171st Machine Gun Coy Feb 1917-Feb 1918		
War Diary	Grantham	10/02/1917	10/02/1917
War Diary	Southampton	11/02/1917	11/02/1917
War Diary	Havre	12/02/1917	14/02/1917
War Diary	Outerstein	15/02/1917	19/02/1917
War Diary	Estaires	20/02/1917	20/02/1917
War Diary	Elbow Farm	21/02/1917	26/02/1917
War Diary	Porta Clous Farm Fleurbaix	27/02/1917	28/02/1917
Miscellaneous	D.A.G 3rd Echelon G.H.Q	02/04/1917	02/04/1917
War Diary	Porta Clous Fm. Fleurbaix	01/03/1917	28/03/1917
War Diary	Porta Clous Farm Fleurbaix	01/04/1917	30/04/1917
Miscellaneous	O.C. 171 Coy MGC	02/06/1917	02/06/1917
War Diary	Armentieres	01/05/1917	31/05/1917
Miscellaneous	HQ. 57th Divn	01/07/1917	01/07/1917
War Diary	Armentieres	07/06/1917	31/07/1917
Miscellaneous	H.Q 57th Divn.	01/09/1917	01/09/1917
War Diary	Armentieres	01/08/1917	04/08/1917
War Diary	Fleurbaix	05/08/1917	31/08/1917
Miscellaneous	O.C. 171 M. S. Coy		
War Diary	Fleurbaix	01/09/1917	16/09/1917
War Diary	La Gorgue	17/09/1917	17/09/1917
War Diary	Busnes	18/09/1917	18/09/1917
War Diary	Estree Blanche	19/09/1917	20/09/1917
War Diary	Fontes	21/09/1917	30/09/1917
War Diary	Norrent Fontes	01/10/1917	18/10/1917
War Diary	Renescure	19/10/1917	19/10/1917
War Diary	Proven	20/10/1917	23/10/1917
War Diary	Elverdinghe (Canal Bank Area)	24/10/1917	24/10/1917
War Diary	Langemark	25/10/1917	31/10/1917
Miscellaneous	HQ 57th Div.	01/12/1917	01/12/1917
War Diary	Langemarck	01/11/1917	02/11/1917
War Diary	Elverdinghe (Solferino Camp)	03/11/1917	06/11/1917
War Diary	Autingues	07/11/1917	30/11/1917
War Diary	Autingues (2f 8.1 Calais 13)	01/12/1917	08/12/1917
War Diary	Putney Camp [x27a 4.6 Sheet 17	09/12/1917	15/12/1917
War Diary	Koekuit	16/12/1917	24/12/1917
War Diary	Marguerite Camp B Q C 0.6 (Sheet 28 N.W.)	25/12/1917	31/12/1917
Miscellaneous	Administrative Instructions Issued With O.O. 65	26/12/1918	26/12/1918
Miscellaneous	O.C. 171 M.G. Coy	01/02/1918	01/02/1918
War Diary	Armentieres	01/01/1918	13/01/1918
War Diary	Steenwerck	14/01/1918	20/01/1918
War Diary	Armentieres	21/01/1918	27/01/1918
War Diary	Steenwerck	28/01/1918	01/02/1918
War Diary	Armentieres	02/02/1918	13/02/1918
War Diary	Estaires	14/02/1918	23/02/1918

WO95/2983/8

57 DIV

171 INFANTRY BDE

BRIGADE MACHINE GUN CORPS

57TH DIVISION
171ST INFY BDE

171ST MACHINE GUN COY.
FEB 1917- FEB 1918

Army Form C. 2118.

171 Company M.E.C.
Vol 1

WAR DIARY or INTELLIGENCE SUMMARY

(Erase heading not required.)

Instructions regarding War Diaries and Intelligence Summaries are contained in F.S. Regs., Part II. and the Staff Manual respectively. Title Pages will be prepared in manuscript.

Place	Date	Hour	Summary of Events and Information	Remarks and references to Appendices
Grantham	10.2.17	9 AM	Left for Southampton by train.	
Southampton	11.2.17	6 AM	Arrived at detraining platform at docks. Transport embarked on "Hunscraft" which sailed at 6 PM. Remainder of company sailed at 8 pm on "Viper". Weather calm. Journey without incident	
Havre	12.2.17	3 AM	Arrived. Marched to docks rest camp. Transport at Halle 3 Grew supplies	
Havre	12.2.17	4 PM	Entrained. Company proceeded by two troop trains via Abbeville, St Omer, Bailleul where detrained. Went into billets at Outersteen.	
	14.2.17			
Outersteen	15.2.17 to 19.2.17		Billeted at Outersteen. Joined 171 Inf. Bde. 57th Division.	
Estaires	20.2.17		Billeted for the night	
Elbow Farm	21.2.17 to 26.2.17		Company took over Boutillerie Sector, relieving 1 New Zealand M.G. Coy. No 3 & 4 Secs in line. two gunners front line, four in close reserve, four in reserve at Coy H.Qrs.	
Porte Close Farm Fleurbaix	27.2.17 28.2.17		Carried out usual firing from front line & indirect fire on enemy's trenches & communications	

A.W. Corbet.
O.C. 171 Coy M.E.C.

2449 Wt. W14957/M90 750,000 1/16 J.B.C. & A. Forms/C.2118/12.

From :- O.C.
   171 Coy.
       M.G.C.

To :- D.A.C.
      3rd Echelon
        G.H.Q.

Herewith War Diary of the 171st M.G. Coy. for the month of March

   J.L. Williams Lieut for Captn.
        Cemdg. 171 M.G Corps.

Army Form C. 2118.

171 Coy M.G.C.

Vol 2

WAR DIARY
or
INTELLIGENCE SUMMARY
(Erase heading not required.)

Instructions regarding War Diaries and Intelligence Summaries are contained in F. S. Regs., Part II. and the Staff Manual respectively. Title Pages will be prepared in manuscript.

Place	Date	Hour	Summary of Events and Information	Remarks and references to Appendices
Pont-a-Clément & Fleurbaix	1/3/17 -4/3/17		Usual programme of indirect fire carried out against enemy trenches and communications. FRANSART and PONT DE PIERRE crossroads received particular attention.	
	5/3/17	9:10 P.M.	1 O.R. wounded by rifle shot.	
	6/3/17 -16/3/17		Trench warfare without particular incidents.	
	12/3/17		2 O.R. wounded by stray rifle shots.	
	15/3/17 -23/3/17		Work carried out on support line splinter proof emplacements for anti raid purposes. Fire average 8,000 rounds per night against system expended on indirect fire.	
	24/3/17	3:00 A.M.	6 Vickers fire was directed against road and trench line P.28.c.5.5.0 – O.R.28.c.8.8.0 in conjunction with road carried out by 171 Brigade. 7000 guns covered right flank of raiding party from emplacements in front line. 21,000 rounds expended.	
	25/3/17		One gun put out of action by enemy machine gun bullets in M.G. casing.	
	26/3/17	12:10 P.M.	1 O.R. wounded by shell splinter during hostile shelling of Fleurbaix.	

G.N. Carter Capt.
O.C. 171 Coy M.G.C.

WAR DIARY or INTELLIGENCE SUMMARY

Army Form C. 2118.

171 M G Coy Sht 3

Place	Date	Hour	Summary of Events and Information	Remarks and references to Appendices
Pt.a Gloria Farm	1.4.17 / 6.4.17		The second programme of indirect fire carried out on PONT DE PIERRE CROSS RDS LE MAISNIL	
	6.4.17		LdR received pledge to ensure surface from shell splints	
	7.4.17 / 8.4.17		Barrage barrage on enemy trenches buy Post were recognised by the enemy & returned heavy shelling	
	9.4.17 / 10.4.17		Nothing of importance Period indirect fire programme was carried out	
	11.4.17		In connection with the raid carried out by the 172 Inf Bde on the night 10/11 our guns created a barrage on the enemy trenches. The new MKIV belt used for the first time appeared to be very satisfactory 32,250 rounds were fired	
	12.4.17 / 13.4.17		Nothing incident to report	
	14.4.17		Our guns formed a barrage in conjunction with raid by 171st Inf Bde 29,750 rounds were fired by 4 guns employed	
	15.4.17 / 16.4.17 / 17.4.17		Usual indirect fire continued — no particular incidents	
	18.4.17 / 19.4.17 / 20.4.17		1 Off wounded 3 ORs killed, 1 OR died of wounds 9 ORs wounded all these casualties were caused by shell fire on Hussar Dump Post H 34 a.	

WAR DIARY
or
INTELLIGENCE SUMMARY

(Erase heading not required.)

Army Form C. 2118.

Place	Date	Hour	Summary of Events and Information	Remarks and references to Appendices
Rocky Glaus Farm	21.4.17 22.4.17		No particular incident	
	23.4.17		Search light noticed at point approx O.19.a.3/9 & extinguished by our Lewis Gun fire from gun at N.5b.d.25/90	
	24.4.17		1 Cpl wounded 20.4.17 died of wounds	
	25.4.17		This company was relieved by 170 Coy M.G.C. in the Bouleversée sector	
	26.4.17		Company transferred to Transport Lt Edwin's Sector relieved by Coy M.G.C.	
	27.4.17		Reconnaissance time was spent in reconnoitering & selecting emplacements & making plans for new emplacements	
	28.4.17 29.4.17 30.4.17		Indirect fire was carried out on various transport roads & rest billets etc	

A.W. [Carter] Capt

From :- OC
   171 Coy
      MGC

To :- HQ

Herewith War Diary
of the 171 MG Coy
for the month of May

F.S.Williams Lieut
a/OC 171 Coy MGC

Army Form C. 2118.

WAR DIARY
or
INTELLIGENCE SUMMARY
(Erase heading not required.)

Instructions regarding War Diaries and Intelligence Summaries are contained in F. S. Regs., Part II. and the Staff Manual respectively. Title Pages will be prepared in manuscript.

No. 171 COY., M.G.C.
No. ....
Date 2.6.17
ORDERLY ROOM

Place	Date	Hour	Summary of Events and Information	Remarks and references to Appendices
German line	1.5.17		In direct fire was carried on enemy roads, tramways	
	2.5.17		reserve of ammunition to trenches. Harassing	
	3.5.17		in report. Average daily expenditure of ammunition being 200	
	to 5.17		rounds.	
			Two O.R.s wounded by shell splinters	
	7.5.17			
	8.5.17		Several new targets picked up from aeroplane photographs	
	9.5.17			
	10.5.17		O.P. wounded by shell splinters	
	11.5.17		Harassing fire of front positions continued. Expenditure been average each	
			gun/teams of ammunition increased to 300 rounds	
	12.5.17		as a result of aeroplane report	
	13.5.17			
	14.5.17		Barrage on enemy strongpoint which was repeatedly brought down	
	15.5.17		The enemy was repeatedly fired during this period. Lewis fire	
	16.5.17		also commenced carried on as before. Average daily expenditure	
	to 21.5.17		of ammunition being 200 rounds	
	22.5.17		Enemy more active. Shelling of back areas took place increasing	
	23.5.17		on our outposts became hotter	
	24.5.17		2nd Lieut. J .... reported from M.G. Base	
	25.5.17		The morale incidents of trench warfare a.g. M.G.s which acting	
	26.5.17		— stopped ally on enemy on every subsidiary line	
	27.5.17			

M G Bace

WAR DIARY or INTELLIGENCE SUMMARY

Army Form C. 2118.

Place	Date	Hour	Summary of Events and Information	Remarks and references to Appendices
Armentières	28.5.17 / 31.5.17		The enemy has shown increasing aerial activity. The shelling this week has stopped. Normal M.G. activity. No unusual incidents to report.	

J.R. Williams Lieut
MGC in M/C Coy

From :- OC
 171 Coy MGC

To :- HQ
 57th Divn

Herewith War Diary of
the 171st M.G. Coy. for the
month of June. 1917.

 A.N. Witts
 Capt.
 Comdg 171 Coy MGC

WAR DIARY
or
INTELLIGENCE SUMMARY

Army Form C. 2118.

Place	Date	Hour	Summary of Events and Information	Remarks and references to Appendices
Armentières	7/6/17		1. OR received wounds in the legs from shell splinters (Senior)	Ammunition Expended 9,700 Rds
—	8.6.17		1 OR received wound in left arm M.G. Bullet	
—	8.6.17		M.Gs more active than usual. Heavy shelling of back areas. Special attention to gun nests & screens at I.31.f 94.73.	Ammunition Expended 8,250 Rds
—	9.6.17		Enemy M.G. Normal. Continued shelling of old town. New target fired on at LA HONGRIE FME. I.11.9/0. — marked absence of Very lights from enemy. O.R. wounded by shell splinter on 7.6.17 died to-day	Ammunition Expended 10,400 Rds
—	10.6.17		Heavy shelling of back areas. Ammunition a gun shelled & hanging occurred behind our lines whilst firing for several hours.	Ammunition Expended 9,500 Rds.
—	11.6.17		Enemy artillery again active on Irish avenue. Shrapnel was sent onto our supports. Back areas & Armentières were heavily shelled. Phosphorous was used by our artillery and several enemy trenches & dug outs gas shelled in anticipation of possible enemy attack.	Ammunition Expended 9000.
—	12.6.17		The Enemy shelled back areas very heavily. Our morning tea was steamed & men shelled for. 2 ORs were wounded. One of them died of wounds.	Ammunition Expended 8,250
—	13.6.17		Nothing unusual to report. Normal activity of machine guns. Shelling of back areas decreased. Enemies aerial activity on both sides	Ammunition Expended 7,250

WAR DIARY
or
INTELLIGENCE SUMMARY

(Erase heading not required.)

Army Form C. 2118.

Place	Date	Hour	Summary of Events and Information	Remarks and references to Appendices
Armentieres	14.6.17		A large fire was observed in the direction of FREELING HEIM from Shaft Farm. Special attention given to TRAMWAY. Shelling of trench areas continued. O.18.a.70/95 - and 95/45	Ammunition Expended 12,750 Rds
"	15.6.17		Considerable aerial activity shown. Mutual indirect fire carried out in 172th & R Sectors. Enemy movement observed by German support line South of Les 4 stillets Farm. C.23.b/40	Ammunition Expended 10,000 Rds
"	16.6.17		Greater aerial & artillery activity shown. Seven enemy observation balloons were up our patrol was destroyed	Ammunition Expended 12,750 Rds
"	17.6.17		Enemy aircraft machine gun active. Rest Camp guest brick Ardicue. Shelled.	Ammunition 13,000 Rds
"	18.6.17		A large fire was visible behind the enemy line in the vicinity of Prez.lon. 1 O.R. wounded by shell fire	Ammunition Expended 12,250
"	19.6.17		Several large fires observed behind enemy lines were observed from Hougham Switch in area of my Barracks at Soncherois 2.6.3 into	Ammunition Expended 10,500 Rds
"	20.6.17		Considerable Artillery activity. Two four capture balloons were destroyed.	Ammunition Expended 8,500 Rds

WAR DIARY
or
INTELLIGENCE SUMMARY

(Erase heading not required.)

Army Form C. 2118.

No. 171 COY., M.G.C. — ORDERLY ROOM

Instructions regarding War Diaries and Intelligence Summaries are contained in F.S. Regs., Part II. and the Staff Manual respectively. Title Pages will be prepared in manuscript.

Place	Date	Hour	Summary of Events and Information	Remarks and references to Appendices
Armentières	21.6.17		Enemy artillery quiet — little hostile M.G. activity — 2 guns fired on front line Kit No. 9 in support raid in daylight in support of raid.	18,500 Rds
"	22.6.17		Enemy artillery increased — increased rifle fire & sniping by the enemy — artillery registered on our supports	7,200 Rds
"	23.6.17		Continued artillery liveliness. Support line shelled in several places. 3 of our observation balloons brought down by enemy planes.	11,300 Rds
"	24.6.17		Artillery activity normal — greate aerial activity.	8,550 Rds
"	25.6.17		Artillery very active on our support line. Enemy aeroplane flew along our entraining line & continuous rattle of machine gun fire. Photograph taken of our new flame gun Tpt by S.P.G. for identification.	6,200 Rds
"	26.6.17		Enemy artillery quiet — greater aerial activity.	6,000 Rds
"	27.6.17		Enemy artillery active during the morning. During night M.G. were very active. Searchlights used to discover four aeroplanes crossing enemy lines.	6,000 Rds
"	28.6.17		Nothing unusual to report.	4,500 Rds
"	29.6.17		Enemy artillery active on our supports — 150 rounds fired at supports. M.G. emplacement at T.9.a.8/90.	4,500 Rds
"	30.6.17		Enemy artillery moderately active — chief targets were Rue Avenue — Battery shoot on our support - line T.9.c.9.7.	4,500 Rds

G. N. Curtis Capt.
O/C 171 Coy M.G.C.

WAR DIARY or INTELLIGENCE SUMMARY

Army Form C. 2118.

171 M.E. Coy R.E.

(Erase heading not required.)

Instructions regarding War Diaries and Intelligence Summaries are contained in F. S. Regs., Part II. and the Staff Manual respectively. Title Pages will be prepared in manuscript.

Place	Date	Hour	Summary of Events and Information	Remarks and references to Appendices
Armentières	1/1/17		Enemy M.G.'s active on advancing by roads near Beck. Area heavily shelled. Trench ports for their firing O.3.d.4.4. CENTRAL DRIVE O.3.a.6.9.4x - C.29.A.75.50 Pudonnaise infantry	57.00
	2/2/17		Very relative at our M.T.M.J. Enemy aircraft very active firing constantly on any lines - 2 continued with J.H.J.M. 2350 rounds were fired on unknown to commencement I.n.c 9.7/4 - 17.7a 4.7c Enemy registered on TOWNGATE C.T.	55.00
	3/2/17		Enemy machine guns most active during heat hours - right - and - mine - left (2 of these were killed at ??)	4,575
	4/2/17		Artillery normally active - M.E.'s quite than usual - Less aeroplane activity - our platoons of level trench in enemy target 6 gas shells reported falling near 25.87	4,10?0
	5/2/17		Enemy guns active a.m. back + wing especially about 9.30 p.m. Enemy Hal. Bly active on Bois bridge, shoot brew + brook Avenue - our artillery party received twin bridges reported to killed 5 gun land on target u Enemy snipers very ready to act on anything	4,000
	6/2/17		Enemy barrage placed on sector truth or g.t.a firing bridges for 5 knell, cannon 12,150 trench No.1 v 3.973 from during the raid on central target 5500 made in support of raid on the right	
	7/2/17		Artillery not so active as usual. Enemy M.G.'s very active in grass land on shrapnel firing rifle grenade apparently exist our right - an unusual amount of rifle fire. No 5 gun fixed in the gap in wire at T.n.b 5.9.4.3 v I.n.b 5.7.2	4,000

2449 Wt. W14957/M90 750,000 1/16 J.B.C. & A. Forms/C.2118/12.

WAR DIARY
or
INTELLIGENCE SUMMARY

(Erase heading not required.)

Army Form C. 2118.

Instructions regarding War Diaries and Intelligence Summaries are contained in F.S. Regs., Part II. and the Staff Manual respectively. Title Pages will be prepared in manuscript.

Place	Date	Hour	Summary of Events and Information	Ammunition Expended	Remarks and references to Appendices
Armentières	8/7/17		2 coys shoot with 172 MG Coy 4 guns fired 5,950 rounds on sniped targets. 1500 rounds expended on 2 gaps in Hienenfortelsen	16,000	
—	9/7/17		Emplacement at the Invers damaged by shell fire. Guns discharged at 1.30 am. Gaps in Heavy F.L. enlarged	14,500	
—	10/7/17		Moderate artillery activity during the day. Heavy shelling of sniped during the night	10,500 rds	
—	11/7/17		Bombing directed on Invers, Tartelages thoroughly by wheel guns slightly damaged, shell fire. 3 ORs killed 10 ORs wounded	12,000 rds	
—	12/7/17		Enemy registered on CAMBRIDGE AVE by day. MGs say active during the nig at. shelled heavy at night	9,000 rds	
—	13/7/17		Turret Gun gun special shots to turn shrill shelter at our wheel front transport lines	9,700 rds	
—	14/7/17		During the day the enemy turned out destructive shell & rifle support fire line of CAMBRIDGE AVE at 8.30 pm from heavy Arty 15 min placed a F.L.	9,000 rds	
—	15/7/17		Sgt Sam & 2 injs a major out put down for retreat in front. hit. miss to N.M.b and new F.L. a reconnaissance both butal millines under M.M transport came 1872 killed by wounded	17,000 rds	

2449 Wt. W14957/M90 750,000 1/16 J.B.C. & A. Forms/C.2118/12.

WAR DIARY
or
INTELLIGENCE SUMMARY

(Erase heading not required.)

Army Form C. 2118.

Place	Date	Hour	Summary of Events and Information	Remarks and references to Appendices
Armentières	16.7.17		Enemy artillery showed considerable activity during the day. Trenches & front line were shelled. 3 separate barrages 8.30pm, 10.25pm, 3.5am.	Amm¹ Exp⁴ 11,500 rds
"	19.7.17		Moderate artillery activity. Brickstack Farm received considerable attention	12,000 rds
"	18.7.17		Support line shelled 10 - 12⁰⁰pm — much quieter generally.	13,000 rds
"	19.7.17		Shelling of back areas took place — Gas released against enemy. Retaliation by T.M. — Iron Ave shelled MGs. Great activity on our Southern line.	13,500 rds
"	20.7.17		Aeroplane heavily shelled. From 12am to 3am many shells placed in neighbourhood of Tunnel gun. Very active shelling of back areas.	13,500 rds
"	21.7.17		Normal activity of artillery during the day. Gas shells sent into support line & communications. Hostile artillery active on back areas.	13,500 rds
"	22.7.17		Enemy placed a barrage on our support trenches during the morning. Trench Mortar gun & River Bat. Special attention by our MGs to gap in wire I 50 c8/25 - I 57A 22/60	13,500 rds

WAR DIARY or INTELLIGENCE SUMMARY

Army Form C. 2118.

Instructions regarding War Diaries and Intelligence Summaries are contained in F.S. Regs., Part II. and the Staff Manual respectively. Title Pages will be prepared in manuscript.

(Erase heading not required.)

Place	Date	Hour	Summary of Events and Information	Remarks and references to Appendices
Armentières	23.7.17		Large proportion of gas shells were sent into our back areas. A systematic shelling of back areas took place.	Ammn Expended 13,000 Rds
—	24.7.17		Ammunition dump shelled with gas shells at 11.15 pm. Masks were used till 1.30 am. — Enemy shelling of back areas.	14,500 Rds
—	25.7.17		A raid was made on German trenches. 19 M.G's operated firing on enemy F.L. & F.L. lines of this raided sector. Two guns were placed in ambush position at enemy front line but did not open fire.	38,000 Rds
—	26.7.17		Renewed shelling of back areas & Armentières. The enemy registered on artillery line near St. Gillers. N° 8 gun tested on new S.O.S. Target. (M.G.M.G.)	11,250 Rds
—	27.7.17		Enemy active on back areas & Armentières during the day: a large quantity of gas shells were discharged against us. 1 O.R. Wounded.	120,000 Rds
—	28.7.17		The enemy shelled Hamel Houplines & Houplines Cambridge lines received special attention 4.2's being dropped along its whole length. 1 O.R. wounded.	—
—	29.7.17		Armentières was heavily shelled at 12.30 am T 2.30 am. with H.E's & Gas Shells. Several direct hits were obtained in the billet occupied by the Company. Two masks were worn throughout bombardment. 1 O.R. wounded. The casualties from gas.	130,000 Rds

Army Form C. 2118.

WAR DIARY
or
INTELLIGENCE SUMMARY

(Erase heading not required.)

Instructions regarding War Diaries and Intelligence Summaries are contained in F. S. Regs., Part II. and the Staff Manual respectively. Title Pages will be prepared in manuscript.

Place	Date	Hour	Summary of Events and Information	Remarks and references to Appendices
Armentières	30.7.17		Fairly active shelling of back areas during the day. The night passed quietly in the lines. More enemy shelling was directed against the area which includes the billets of this company. 1 O.R. was killed & 4 O.Rs wounded. As a result of the projectile by means of gas shells 1 Officer & 15 O.Rs were admitted to hospital.	Ammunition 120000 Rds
"	31.7.17		Hostile shelling of back areas not so active as usual. Indirect fire on I.11.d 15.9.2 in connection with Gas Trench Raid.	13. 5000 Rds

J.H. Wells Lieut A/O.C.
17. M.G. Coy.

From
O.C. 171 M.G. Coy
To
H.Q. 57th Divn.

Herewith War Diary of the 171st M.G. Coy
for the month of August, '17.

A. Blackman Lt.
(for) O.C. 171 M.G. Coy

WAR DIARY or INTELLIGENCE SUMMARY

Army Form C. 2118.

171 M G Coy

Place	Date	Hour	Summary of Events and Information	Remarks and references to Appendices
Armentieres	1/8/17		Hostile artillery was active. Hostile M.G's were quiet.	Ammn Expended 8,500 Rds
"	2/8/17		Enemy artillery quiet. M G's & aircraft were inactive.	12,000 rds
"	3/8/17		Hostile shelling attack areas renewed during the night. The relief of the 61st Divn completed.	4,500
"	4/8/17		Hostile artillery active on front support lines track area. M G's active after 9.15pm. Relief of No 3 section completed.	3,000
Linsown	5/8/17		Bombs dropped by enemy aeroplanes behind our lines. Trench Mortars from sudden fire first responded.	3,000
"	6/8/17		Artillery active between Tenbown & Bay Ave. Considerable damage done to support trenches also MG trenches	3,000
"	7/8/17		No unusual incident to report — generally quiet.	3,000

WAR DIARY
or
INTELLIGENCE SUMMARY

(Erase heading not required.)

Army Form C. 2118.

Instructions regarding War Diaries and Intelligence Summaries are contained in F. S. Regs., Part II. and the Staff Manual respectively. Title Pages will be prepared in manuscript.

Place	Date	Hour	Summary of Events and Information	Remarks and references to Appendices
Hondun	8/8/17		Hostile artillery more active. Shelling support line between Crête Penney Ave suggested registration.	Ammn Expended 3000 rds.
—	9/8/17		M.G's very active on Rue David — more aerial activity.	3000 rds
—	10/8/17		Heavy bombardment on our right. A great many observation balloons were in use.	3000 rds.
—	11/8/17		Enemy machine guns active traversing our support lines	3,000 rds.
—	12/8/17		Not so many enemy M.G's have fired during the past 24 hrs & different targets have been engaged. An observation balloon ascended opposite this sector	3,000 rds.
—	13/8/17		Enemy rushed Gap between Posts No 1 & No 2 our No 2 Gun fired 1000 rounds into the Gap in response to Request of Infantry Officer. Two balloons ascended opposite this sector	6,500 rds.

WAR DIARY
or
INTELLIGENCE SUMMARY

Army Form C. 2118.

Instructions regarding War Diaries and Intelligence Summaries are contained in F. S. Regs., Part II. and the Staff Manual respectively. Title Pages will be prepared in manuscript.

Place	Date	Hour	Summary of Events and Information	Remarks and references to Appendices
FLEURBAIX	14/8/17		Slight increase in enemy artillery activity. HUDSON BAY came in for trench strafing. Visibility good & our aircraft consequently active. Hostile a/c machine-gunned to object to & fired at from an anti-aircraft gun of the front trench enemy front-line.	2000 rds.
do.	15/8/17		Enemy artillery inactive except in response to our trench-mortar shoots. Our machine-guns apart from the usual indirect fire fired 2,250 rds stopping fire in another to an S.O.S. sent up by the Portuguese. A peculiar thing of the day was the unusual inactivity on the part of enemy machine-guns & however not the crew of a relief in his front.	4,250 rds.
do.	16/8/17		Artillery on both sides exceedingly quiet. Enemy active in the air heavy engaged by our anti-aircraft guns without result. Enemy machine-guns resumed their normal activity, but fairly concentrated rather than traversing fire. Two new machine-guns had in getting on to the heart, but fired near FLAG ALLEY again fired in response to the Portuguese S.O.S.	2,450 rds.
do.	17/8/17		Hostile artillery continued to back area work. Enemy aircraft busy during day & night when they were picked up by a searchlight & heavily engaged by our 'archies' without result. Machine-guns fire normal during day. Our own machine guns sent to fire into enemy front-line trench during the night in response to S.O.S. sent up by the Portuguese.	4,650 rds.

WAR DIARY or INTELLIGENCE SUMMARY

Army Form C. 2118.

Place	Date	Hour	Summary of Events and Information	Remarks and references to Appendices
FLEURBAIX	18/8/17		Hostile artillery was engaged in sundry – battery work no other. Our front line with the exception of HUDSON BAY Posts in the air in both salts was less than usual, however the enemy trench mortars were active from after 9 p.m. Enemy machine guns (especially our new front line in clear) to Pentangle S.O.S. front opposite our front line in clear to Pentangle S.O.S.	Ammunition Expenditure 2,250 rds
do.	19/8/17		HUDSON BAY & PINNEYS AVENUE lights pulled away the enemy and a few bombs were put into the track at rear. Our own artillery was more active. A gas projector attack was made near the BRIDOUX SALIENT, no retaliation from the enemy. Hostile aircraft (very few in no.) dropped a few bombs during the night. Our aircraft & our own lewis guns were specially active & put up attacks. Firing at Portugal S.O.S. Our right gun platoon on Stratford Rd. opposite to Portugal. Was fired on by Portugal.	3,000 rds.
do.	20/8/17		HUDSON BAY POST & BAY AVENUE were shelled with trench mortars throwing to the white enemy artillery more. Enemy aircraft active. About 11:30 p.m. their bombing machines were active few bombs were dropped round DEAD DOG DUMP in the direct hit being obtained. Enemy machine guns more active. Our own enemy and normal programme of indirect fire.	2,000 rds.
do.	21/8/17		Increased enemy artillery activity. FORAY HOUSE (Battn. H.Q.) was heard shelled. The Inhabitants forced to evacuate. Returning shell-fire not so much about ELBOW FARM and TIN BARN TRAH. Enemy aircraft very active during the night; few bombs were dropped (by Ed?) in the vicinity of Reg. D2 (Bois). Enemy machine guns active especially on the early morning. Night (Oct?) sub-sector quiet.	300 rds.

2449 Wt. W14957/M90 750,000 1/16 J.B.C. & A. Forms/C.2118/12.

Army Form C. 2118.

WAR DIARY or INTELLIGENCE SUMMARY
(Erase heading not required.)

Place	Date	Hour	Summary of Events and Information	Remarks and references to Appendices
				Ammunition Expenditure
FLEURBAIX	22/8/17		On the Left Sub-sector enemy artillery was active during the day paying special attention to the HUDSON BAY POST & BAY AVENUE. Enemy machine-guns normal. Activity in the air was considerable. Bombing planes crossed our lines twice engaged by anti-aircraft guns, aided by searchlights, with no results. At 4 p.m. a small yellow floated toy balloon came to earth near NYE FARM it had attached pamphlets. Round type. Our machine-guns carried out usual indirect fire programme. Trench fire in response to Portuguese S.O.S. Left Sub-sector quiet.	3,000 rds.
do.	23/8/17		A quiet day on 11th Sub-sector. However between 1.10 a.m. & 2 a.m. the enemy put down a concentrated barrage on our support & front line trenches HUDSON BAY & CONVENT AVENUE. At the same time the enemy raided with a party of 2 officers & men but stopping machine-guns rendered the front line untenable to the enemy & killed 4 officers in no man's land in front of support line. Two of our emplacements were slightly damaged & 1 O.R. was killed. No Portuguese troops attained (the six guns firing got off 14,250 rds. in another 2,000 rds. were expended in indirect fire) Right side Left Sub-sector quiet at 11.30 p.m. the enemy guns not possible.	16,250 rds.
do.	24/8/17		Both sectors very quiet. Visibility very poor owing to overcast weather in the air. No balloons put in an appearance. Our machine-guns carried out usual programme of indirect fire, and fire was also opened in response to a Portuguese S.O.S.	3,250 rds.

WAR DIARY or INTELLIGENCE SUMMARY

Army Form C. 2118.

Place	Date	Hour	Summary of Events and Information	Remarks and references to Appendices
FLEUR BAIX	25/8/17		Enemy artillery more or less inactive on both fronts — sector in general very quiet today. In the air active and seven of our planes — Enemy machine guns were rather especially between 5 & 9 p.m. Our guns carried out normal programme of indirect fire.	Ammunition Expenditure 3,000 rds.
do.	26/8/17		Enemy artillery quiet all day. Two hostile machine guns showed a marked activity in taking pot shots aircraft, putting up a real barrage in front of our planes. It was a great test of perception but for machine guns carried out normal programme of indirect fire on enemy's rear trench system roads.	3,000 rds.
do.	27/8/17		Bad weather conditions made things very difficult for the artillery and also aircraft, the inadequate light having an especial[ly] good day on both Brit. & Ger. sides. His machine-guns did not fire a shot all day, ours carried out the normal programme of indirect fire.	2,000 rds
do.	28/8/17		Bad weather conditions again prevented carrying on artillery + aerial activities on both sides. Trench-mortars more than usually active, over L.T.M.B.'s put over 30 no. opposite TIN BARN AVE. During the night the enemy machine guns were exceptionally active in the sector, his the right the CORDONNERIE LEFT as well Bombardment took place between 11.30 pm & 12.15 am. Our artillery quickly replied. His machine guns active as usual & indirect fire.	3,000 rds
do.	29/8/17		Weather conditions made aerial patrolling activity almost nil like enemy threw 20 77 mm S. near BOND ST. Enemy machine guns were traversing our support line; our guns carried out normal indirect fire.	3,000 rds.

WAR DIARY or INTELLIGENCE SUMMARY

Army Form C. 2118.

(Erase heading not required.)

Place	Date	Hour	Summary of Events and Information	Ammunition Expenditure	Remarks and references to Appendices
FLEURBAIX	30/8/17		Enemy artillery inactive. A few shells being fired into the back areas in the night. Our S.O.S. and standing barrages have been immensely from hostile shelling for a considerable period, but trench mortars carried on a short shoot from the night of DEMN WE. Period active. Slight missing of weather - everything of our machine guns carried out normal programme of indirect fire.	3000 rds.	
do	31/8/17		At 4.30 pm our trench-mortars carried out a shoot from the left Sub-Sector to which enemy replied with trench mortars on our front line & whizz-bangs on the supports. Very little activity observed. Our artillery fired actively at intervals during day firing on rear of Enemy Support Line. Despite good weather, conditions, enemy aircraft were inactive over our lines in contrast to patrolling the front line all day. At 12.15 am three of our planes crossed over our lines & dropped lights in the enemy front line system. Our machine guns fired on targets in rear of enemy front line as normal.	3000 rds.	

MBlackman 2Lt
(A) O.C. 171 M.G. Coy.

From / O.C. 171 M.S. Co.
To / H.Q. 54th Div.

Herewith War Diary for the month
of September, 1917.

M Blackman Lt
(for) O.R. 171 M.S. Co.

WAR DIARY or INTELLIGENCE SUMMARY

Army Form C. 2118.

171 M.G. Coy

Place	Date	Hour	Summary of Events and Information	Remarks and references to Appendices
Flesquières	1/9/17		Enemy artillery quiet - very little activity of any kind shown by the enemy but stopping gun fires on our own F.L. in response to S.O.S. signal. Expending 2000 rds.	5000 rds
—	2/9/17		Little enemy artillery activity. Hostile aeroplane dropped bombs on back areas to the N. of this sector	3000 rds
—	3/9/17		Enemy artillery still inactive. No machine guns showed increased activity on our support & communication trenches. Our artillery opened out at 12.15am on red night being sent up to the right of No.6 position.	3000 rds.
—	4/9/17		Artillery cooperated quiet on 171 sector. Enemy machine guns active 16 right. Two machine gun camps at 1 the mounds programme of indirect fire. About activity in hot belo sniper to Saturday.	3000 rds.
—	5/9/17		Artillery on this sector fit not active. Very round enemy active enemy machine guns active in the left sub-sector and on the right flanged this target. But one action in this direction have looked to being a tramways funds in view of a possible relief. Outposts the infantry sent out 16 men on a silent raid of returned with 2 prisoners. Hostile air active marked silence anti-aircraft guns troy.	3000 rds

Army Form C. 2118.

WAR DIARY
or
INTELLIGENCE SUMMARY
(Erase heading not required.)

Instructions regarding War Diaries and Intelligence Summaries are contained in F.S. Regs., Part II. and the Staff Manual respectively. Title Pages will be prepared in manuscript.

Place	Date	Hour	Summary of Events and Information	Remarks and references to Appendices
FLEURBAIX	6/9/17		Enemy artillery fairly at present - trench-mortars & rifles sent not typical and Enemy trench-mortars firing in the kinds of day C.B.C. Enemy machine-guns more active. Our artillery was active in intense bursts of fire. Our machine-guns carried out normal indirect fire programme of 2160 [?] rounds 1000 rds in response to an S.O.S. at 11.40 pm & not the "all clear" was reported	Ammunition expended 4000 rds
do.	7/9/17		Enemy artillery material inactive. Few machine-guns fired but played. Trench sapping as last night. Our trench mortars active & silenced an enemy mortar & silent. Our own artillery silenced enemy T.M. Bombarded temporarily with trench mortars to a strategy area AVE. Denis(?) MOC Section no. 9 of airplane of RADINGHEM + Fauquissart NRS enemy arc. Our machine-guns carried out indirect fire as usual.	3000 rds.
do.	8/9/17		Enemy artillery inactive except owing to normal hostilities. The machine guns swept our unused rails, first during the night. Our own artillery carried out short reports as yesterday. Few M. Guns. Our machine-guns fired and usual indirect fire. Our trench-mortars active and 4 separate shoots without retaliation.	2600 rds.
do.	9/9/17		Enemy artillery slightly more active in response to our airborne Enemy trench-mortars active. Our MG's also silenced two rounds from 3 p - 8 p - 10.15 p. Guns Plane enemy arc rounds of time at 3 p - 8 p - 10.15 p.	3000 rds.
do.	10/9/17		Enemy artillery more active. The Sellum to not falling with "moaning minnies" Our guns were active. Our artillery carried out normal shoots as well as one French- mortars (Y-gun). Our machine guns carried out usual harrass. 12 midnight + 2 am. At 3 am airplane replied with gunfire usual enemy trenches night flying on fifth side before. 9.40 pm	3000 rds.

2449 Wt. W14957/M90 750,000 1/16 J.B.C. & A. Forms/C.2118/12.

WAR DIARY or INTELLIGENCE SUMMARY

Army Form C. 2118.

Place	Date	Hour	Summary of Events and Information	Remarks and references to Appendices
FLEURBAIX	11/9/17		Our artillery activity until little reply from the enemy with the exception of some "minnenwerfer" shells on our front line stations & on 9pm Pineapple shots thrown over from trench mortar. Enemy machine guns as well as rifle normally active. Few trench mortar shots encountered.	3,000 rds
do.	12/9/17		Artillery & M.G. activity. Machine gunners on fifth street harassed. Of great aid I was has been seen from the new line, some times engines and signs having occasionally been heard, very plainly too, and various jet lights seen supposing that these lights have worked out to silent lines heard.	3,700 rds
do.	13/9/17		Enemy artillery exchanged greater activity than to be making most use of his trench mortars on our front line system. At 9pm shells were fired in the direction of LAVENTIE. His artillery was active during the afternoon from 9am-1.30. E.S.L. into street, from 5pm my tile my tiles & various shells E.S.L & E.S.L. Machine gun activity normal to Patt shells	3,200 rds
do.	14/9/17		Enemy trench mortar active during the day. At 6.30 am a flying pig shot was seen & the enemy trench mortars firing heavy harassing fire. Rifle battery active. A gun light ROUGE DE BOOT firing to morning. At 11.25pm a Green light the S.O.S signal, N.2/35, NO2 gun fired 40 rds as required the S.O.S pitched to be a mistake. At 1am a green light was sent up from BOND ST, no2 gun fired 100 rds. 1 hour fell around my guns. At 4.30am a considerable range of no jello fell around my batteries in a tin lunge and could have reached NB7 and NMINE AVE also in action during the night the night gunfire was successful. Hostile aircraft were hammered all	11,567 rds

WAR DIARY or INTELLIGENCE SUMMARY

Army Form C. 2118.

Place	Date	Hour	Summary of Events and Information	Remarks and references to Appendices
FLEURBAIX	15/9/17		On the left Sub-Sector enemy artillery active in and support line near FLAG ALLEY. An enemy plane "Sputting" mainly "Minnies" were sent at pgts beyond being the CWs. 6 planes attempted to cross our lines but were driven off. Machine guns on both sides normal. The state of our trench after the recent rains is gun shooting in the case of sealing rifles.	
FLEURBAIX	16/9/17		The company was relieved by nightfall by 11th M.G.Ey. A march was made to billets at LA GORGUE. Nothing of importance happened during the day.	
LA GORGUE	17/9/17		The day was spent in cleaning up and preparing for the march on the morrow.	
BUSNES	18/9/17		The company took part in a brigade march to BUSNES where billets were taken up in the afternoon. No parades were made for a further march on the morrow.	
ESTREE BLANCHE	19/9/17		A further march was made to ESTREE BLANCHE and billets taken over.	
do.	20/9/17		The day was spent in cleaning up generally.	
FONTES	21/9/17		Billets were cleaned out during the morning. Kits were given in during the afternoon that we went to hunt to FONTES. The rest was carried out and billets taken over.	
do.	22/9/17		The day was spent on addition of cleaning up of billets.	
do.	23/9/17		Check parade & further cleaning up.	
do.	24/9/17		Training project commenced. Squad drill, range-drill, P.T., &c.	
do.	25/9/17		Training programme continued. Special attention being paid to range work.	

Army Form C. 2118.

WAR DIARY
or
INTELLIGENCE SUMMARY

(Erase heading not required.)

Instructions regarding War Diaries and Intelligence Summaries are contained in F. S. Regs., Part II. and the Staff Manual respectively. Title Pages will be prepared in manuscript.

Place	Date	Hour	Summary of Events and Information	Remarks and references to Appendices
FINTES	26/9/17		Ordinary Company training conducted.	
	27/9/17		do.	
	28/9/17		do. including range work.	
	29/9/17		do.	
	30/9/17		do.	

M Shadowm ?
for O.C. 171 M.G. Coy

2449 Wt. W14957/M90 750,000 1/16 J.B.C. & A. Forms/C.2118/12.

Army Form C. 2118.

WAR DIARY
or
INTELLIGENCE SUMMARY

171 M G Coy
Vol 9

(Erase heading not required.)

Place	Date	Hour	Summary of Events and Information	Remarks and references to Appendices
NURRENT - FONTES	1/10/17		Company training was carried out, 6 hrs per day. Special attention was given throughout to Barrage Drill and indirect fire work.	
	2/10/17			
	3/10/17			
	4/10/17			
	5/10/17			
	6/10/17		The brigade was inspected by Sir Douglas Haig C.I.C. and ESTREE BLANCHE at 10.30 a.m.	
	7/10/17		Company training continued.	
	8/10/17		A brigade attack was practised near ENGUINEGATTE in which this company took part.	
	9/10/17		Company training continued.	
	10/10/17		An experimental barrage was put down by all the M.G. companies in the division. Rifles were carried and it extended to a depth of 13,000 rounds were expended by this company.	
	11/10/17			
	12/10/17			
	13/10/17		Further company training as above.	
	14/10/17			
	15/10/17			
	16/10/17			
	17/10/17			
	18/10/17			
RENESCURE	19/10/17		The company left billets at 9 a.m. to march with the 141st Inf. Bde. to RENESCURE. The march was accomplished without incident, billets being reached at 3 p.m. There were no stragglers.	

WAR DIARY
or
INTELLIGENCE SUMMARY
(Erase heading not required.)

Army Form C. 2118.

Place	Date	Hour	Summary of Events and Information	Remarks and references to Appendices
~~FROVEN~~ PROVEN	20.10.17		The company entrained and started off at 10 a.m. for PROVEN (OSTEND). Settled in tillets by 3 p.m. at PEGNELL CAMP 1000x S.R.W. in Haringhen (Sheet HAZEBROUCK 5A). 2nd transport and brigades entrained and arrived at tillets by 9 p.m. Leaving Starter from RENESCURE at 9 a.m.	
	21.10.17 22.10.17 23.10.17		Cleaning up in general was carried out. Company training was proceeded with. Company training - stopping practice barrage - drill &c. 2/Lt LANTHIER and 16 O.R. proceeded to XIV Corps Reinforcement Camp, HERZEELE. This party was the 12½% of the gunners to be left out of a projected attack, another 12½% being machinest to remain at our warm lines.	
		4 p.m.	The remainder of the company less transport entrained at PROVEN detrained at ELVERDINGHE - marched to SOLFERINO CAMP (Sheet 28 NW 1/20,000 B22 b 6/4). Transport moved by road to BRIDGE CAMP B30 a 7/5 Sheet 28NW 1/20,000	
ELVERDINGHE (CANAL BANK AREA)	24.10.17		Fighting kit was worn with Company moved at 11 a.m. VIA BARDS CAUSEWAY to LANGEMARK. The 16 guns then took up a position on a line U 18 b 6/7 to V 13 c 2/7 Sheet SCHAAP - BAILE 1/40,000 to put down offensive/protective + S.O.S. Barrage. Advanced Cg HQrs established at DROP HOUSE U 23 c 2/1 Sheet Boesinghe 1/15,000	

WAR DIARY or INTELLIGENCE SUMMARY

Army Form C. 2118.

Place	Date	Hour	Summary of Events and Information	Remarks and references to Appendices
LANGEMARCK	25.10.17		Barrage fire commenced at ZERO hour 5.40 am – 50,000 rounds being expended – Barrage continued for 2 hrs 40 mins. Casualties – 6 O.R. wounded	
do	26.10.17		No 4 Secn. moved to new position V.7.b 9/9 – 9/9. No 3 Secn – one gun to V.8.c 9/0 – 9/0. One gun to V.14.c 2/0 – 2/0. One gun to V.13.d 80/90. One gun to V.14.c 40/30. The other 8 guns remained in SOS barrage positions. Firing NIL. Casualties. 1 O.R. killed. 10 O.R. wounded.	
do	27.10.17		Position of guns remained the same – firing NIL – Casualties 5. O.Rs Wounded	
do	28.10.17		One gun of No 4 Secn was moved from V.7.b 9/9 – 9/9 to V.7.c 9/45. No 3 Secn gun at V.13.d 80/80 was moved to V.13.b 15/25. Firing NIL. Casualties 1 O.R. Wounded	
do	29.10.17		2 guns No 4 Secn were withdrawn from the line to FUSILIER HOUSE — CANAL BANK. 2 guns of No 1 Secn were moved up from V.18.b.6/7 – V.13.c 2/7 to V.7.c 95/15 + V.7.b 9/9 – 9/9. The other two guns of No 1 Secn were also withdrawn & sent to FUSILIER HOUSE. Firing NIL. Casualties. 1 O.R. wounded.	
do	30.10.17		Position 8 guns unchanged. Two of No 1 guns fired from barrage positions in conjunction with Harris. No results observed. One gun of No 3 Sectn at REQUETE FARM V.14.c 5.9 (SCHAAP-BALIE) was destroyed by shell-fire & all ammunition, shell — the position constants under barrage makeing communication difficult. 5.O.R. wounded. No 3 Sectn relieved by No 4 Sectn.	

WAR DIARY
or
INTELLIGENCE SUMMARY

Place	Date	Hour	Summary of Events and Information	Remarks and references to Appendices
LANGEMARK	31.10.17		Barrage on forward area frequent. Enemy aeroplanes busy shooting down into our Shell-holes. Another gun rendered useless by hostile shelling in SENEGAL FARM V7e 9.2 (SERAAP-BOIE). A number of gas-shells were thrown over during the night with small effect. Loads came up for wool supplies by night. No. 1 Reserve Coy came out on relief-section relief, the trucks hour post bus standing to FUSILIER HOUSE. 1 O.R. killed. 3 O.R. wounded.	

W.Mackman 2/Lt
(m) O.C. D. T.M.B. (?)

To:- HQ
    57th Divn.

Herewith original copy of
War Diary of this Company for
the month of November please

[signature] O.C.
171 Coy M.G.C.

171 M.G. Coy
Vol 10

WAR DIARY or INTELLIGENCE SUMMARY

Army Form C. 2118.

Place	Date	Hour	Summary of Events and Information	Remarks and references to Appendices
LANGEMARCK	1.11.17		Hostile artillery very active. Frequent barrages were put down on our front line & shell-holes and on LANGEMARCK ROAD. The troops were shelled all night by enemy artillery. Stringent machine gun fire on 17th Sides was inactive. Enemy aeroplanes appeared above our lines & fired down indiscriminately into our shell-holes. During the night gun-shells caused us some trouble. No casualties.	
do.	2.11.17		Hostile barrages frequent as detailed. Any guns in the front line undamaged. Great difficulty found in the efficient supply of S.A.A. to forward positions. Personnel with the guns in state of fatigue and limited to 4 men per gun team. Company relief by 142 M.G. Coy commenced at 4 p.m. armed in during a hostile gun shell barrage. SOLFERINO CAMP (Sheet 28NW 1/B22-6/4) $\frac{2}{100}$ taken over by all gun-teams under convoy by 2 a.m. 3.11.17.	
ELVERDINGHE (Solferino Camp)	3.11.17		Day spent in cleaning of guns and of men.	
do.	4.11.17		Further cleaning up. Special attention given to men's feet.	
do.	5.11.17		Repacking of limbers & general reorganization. Baths obtained for men at ELVERDINGHE.	
do.	6.11.17		Preparations made for leaving the area. Camp handed over and conference guided at 5.15 p.m. March to entraining point at INTERNATIONAL CORNER (28NW A9c 3.4) Then joined by our transport and Batt l (Battalion transport given by 171 L.T.M.B. who travelled with no. 1 train convoy to. Pandeteene a Peruvian transport given by 171 L.T.M.B. who travelled with no. 1 train convoy to start until 2 a.m. next morning.	

Army Form C. 2118.

WAR DIARY
or
INTELLIGENCE SUMMARY.
(Erase heading not required.)

Instructions regarding War Diaries and Intelligence Summaries are contained in F. S. Regs., Part II. and the Staff Manual respectively. Title pages will be prepared in manuscript.

Place	Date	Hour	Summary of Events and Information	Remarks and references to Appendices
AUTINGUES	7.11.17		Detrained at AUDRUICQ (2A 95.50 HAZEBROUCK 5A) Proceeded by lorries to AUTINGUES (2F B.1 CALAIS 13). Transport followed on road. Took over billets and established Company Headquarters	
do.	8.11.17		Day spent in cleaning up. Particular attention was paid to cleaning of mens clothing & tidying of billets. The temporary O.C. 65 LT H.J. GOLDSPINK proceeded on leave and 2/LT N. BLACKMAN assumed command of the Company	
do.	9.11.17		Further cleaning-up. Packs haversacks scrubbed & billets cleaned.	
do.	10.11.17		Training proper commenced. Wet weather kept men to their billets doing Gun cleaning, Stoppages, Hesterious, Drill in Barrage-Drill &c. Physical training in the afternoon. I believe the N.C.O.s by the O.C. on "Points to be attained in coming training"	
do.	11.11.17		Being Sunday, no training. Church Parade 2.30 pm.	
do.	12.11.17		Training continued. N.C.Os lecture "Faults to be remedied as shown in actual barrage put down by the Coy during the recent operation Gas drill & judging distances (checked by range finder) added to the programme of 10th inst	
do.	13.11.17		Training included "Use of Ground", Cover by practical demonstration. The aiv rifles paraded under the signalling Cpl for instruction	

Army Form C. 2118.

WAR DIARY
or
INTELLIGENCE SUMMARY.
(Erase heading not required.)

Instructions regarding War Diaries and Intelligence Summaries are contained in F. S. Regs., Part II. and the Staff Manual respectively. Title pages will be prepared in manuscript.

Place	Date	Hour	Summary of Events and Information	Remarks and references to Appendices
Autingues	14.11.17.		One hour given to Visual Training - Initiation & Recognition of Targets" Lecture to NCOs in whole Coy. The Censorship Regulations & their purpose. Rangefinders tested their instruments & made range cards attack & defence	
do.	15.11.17.		The usual programme of training was continued & included Drill with auxiliary mounting. Lecture to the whole Coy. on M.G's in the attack.	
do.	16.11.17.		The daily FMO Inspection Parade - Physical Training - Barrage drill - elementary mechanism	
do.	17.11.17.		Inspection of Box Respirators by Gas N.C.O. - Barrage drill F.M.O. Inspection - Gun cleaning & belt filling.	
do.	18.11.17.		Sunday - no training programme. - Church parade	
do.	19.11.17.		The usual items of training. Attacked infantry practised carrying for two hours with Yukon Packs & Jump lines.	
do.	20.11.17.		Lecture to N.C.O's on firing at aircraft". The daily FMO Inspection Barrage drill & elementary machine gun training. Attacked men practised in carrying with Yukon Pack & Jump lines for 1½ hrs.	

WAR DIARY
or
INTELLIGENCE SUMMARY.
(Erase heading not required.)

Army Form C. 2118.

Place	Date	Hour	Summary of Events and Information	Remarks and references to Appendices
Autingues	21.11.17		Special attention given to cleaning & clothing & equipment. Semaphore drill & usual items of N.C.O training.	Gas drill
do	22.11.17		Tactical exercises under sectional arrangements were carried out. Lecture to men on "Use of entering & engineering tools." Lecture given to N.C.O's on "Writing of Reports & messages." Attached men continued practice in carrying.	
do	23.11.17		F.M.O Inspection. Whole Coy paraded for bath at NIELLES	
do	24.11.17		Route march to Range with fighting limbers. Firing on B Range. (a) Ranging (b) Intervening (c) Coming into action & firing at Plates.	
do	25.11.17		Sunday - No training - Church Parade.	
do	26.11.17		Tactical exercises under sectional arrangements (a)taking positions (b)Sanitary map reading (c)Conventional signs (d)Contours. The other usual training continued.	
do	27.11.17		Inspection of Coy by G.O.C Division at 11 am. at in vicinity of billets. Afternoon devoted to same of deficiencies of small kit & checking of Section Stores	
do	28.11.17		(a)Practice in Carrying (b)selection of positions (c)Coming into action. The daily F.M.O. Inspection parade - special attention devoted to Semaphore	
do	29.11.17		The usual training programme continued.	
do	30.11.17		Lecture to N.COs on the use of aiming post & Zero post on barrage fire. Kit inspection & issue of deficiencies. Gas drill	

W Shackman ?
(b)O.C. 171 M.S.Coy

WAR DIARY
or
INTELLIGENCE SUMMARY.
(Erase heading not required.)

Army Form C. 2118.

171 - M.G. Coy

Place	Date	Hour	Summary of Events and Information	Remarks and references to Appendices
AUTINGVES E2F.81 OR.29.15.13 J	1/12/17		Company Training, General Inspection P.T., Gun Drill, Gun - cleaning, Kit Inspection, Lecture by Section Officers on General Routine. Attached infantry promised under the Transport Officer in carrying with Water Fuel and Supplies.	
"	2/12/17		No training. Church Parade at 2.30 p.m.	
"	3/12/17		Mounted Company Training vs. General Inspection P.T., Gun Drill and Mechanism, Range Drill, Lecture on "Esté Gaz", Lecture by Second Lieutenant Post. Attached infantry promised in carrying.	
"	4/12/17		Four hours route march with fighting limbers. Packed in Range Lecture and Lecture on lessons learnt from recent operations. Whilst route-march was in progress the officers carried out a tactical Scheme in the 171st Bde. Training Area.	
"	5/12/17		Company took part in a practice Brigade attack in the 171st Bde. Training Area.	
"	6/12/17		General Company Inspection. Preparations for move of Transport, packing Limbers etc.	
"	7/12/17		Transport joined Brigade Column and commenced trek for PROVEN (OSTEND). Rest of the Company continued training and made further preparations for move.	
"	8/12/17		Company entrained at 8 a.m. and arrived at destination POTIJZE CAMP x 27 a 4.6 (Sheet 12) at 3 p.m. Transport joined the Company at 6 p.m. bringing with it the only draught Horses billetted in barns and under Canvas first Rate Trip.	

Army Form C. 2118.

WAR DIARY
or
INTELLIGENCE SUMMARY.
(Erase heading not required.)

Instructions regarding War Diaries and Intelligence Summaries are contained in F.S. Regs., Part II. and the Staff Manual respectively. Title pages will be prepared in manuscript.

Place	Date	Hour	Summary of Events and Information	Remarks and references to Appendices
PUTNEY CAMP (X21a4.6 Sheet 19.)	9.12.17		Day spent in straightening up the camp, ceremonial inspection, P.T., and drill. Work commenced on covering over latrines and improvements to latrines.	
"	10.12.17		Improvements continued. Normal Company Inspection, P.T., and Squad Drill	
"	11.12.17		Company training continued. 1 N.C.O. & 4 men sent to ELVERDINGHE to draw Nissen Huts for erection of new camp alongside present one.	
"	12.12.17		Ceremonial Inspection, P.T., etc. During the morning the camp was inspected by the Divisional General Major-General R.M.R. Blacker. In the afternoon Lt. H.J. Pittefsick (Temp. O.C.) and 2/Lt A.D.S. Brown proceeded with the N.C.O.s to ELVERDINGHE where they were to be met by guides for the purpose of reconnoitring routes and the new part of the line (HOULTHURST)	
"	13.12.17		Party sent up at 7am to draw more Nissen huts from ELVERDINGHE. Ceremonial Inspection, P.T., Belt-filling, etc. Site cut out for new camp. Reconnoitring party returned.	
"	14.12.17		Work commenced on new camp. Good progress made. Fatigue party of 50 employed from 8.30 am till 4.15 pm. Rest of the company continued with training.	
"	15.12.17		Work continued on new camp during the morning. In the afternoon the company went to LE COUTHOVE CHATEAU for hot baths & change of clothing. Final preparations made for impending move.	

WAR DIARY
or
INTELLIGENCE SUMMARY.

Army Form C. 2118.

Place	Date	Hour	Summary of Events and Information	Remarks and references to Appendices
ROEKUIT	16.12.17		At 8.30 a.m. 11 gun-teams and Headquarters marched from camp to the line. They entrained at PROVEN for BOESINGHE. At about 17.00 they relieved 55 M.G. Coy in the front line of the ROEKUIT Sector. Company Headquarters were established at SIGNAL FARM U.21.c.20.05 (BIXSCHOOTE). The remainder of the company including transport remained at PUTNEY CAMP (CROMBEKE)	
do.	17.12.17		Remainder of Company left for ELVERDINGHE transport by train under the 2i/c 2nd Lt H. BLACKMAN. On arrival rear H.Q. was established at LARRY CAMP B.9.c.2.4 (Sheet 28 N.W.) and transport both over from S.S. M.S. Coy at BLACKHOOD CAMP A.5.c.6.2 (Sheet 28 N.W.) In the line hostile artillery was moderately active shelling roads near our gun-positions. This thought to be due to further this machine guns were also busy firing indirect on to road by EGYPT HOUSE U.12.b.25.90 (BIXSCHOOTE) The gun at FAIDHERBE X ROADS (U.5.d.3.4) was under heavy artillery fire all day. An enemy aeroplane was brought down behind the CANAL BANK during the day. Our anti-aircraft gun stationed at RED HOUSES (U.5d.9.2) put out of action by a shell.	
do.	18.12.17		A quiet day on both sides. Usual desultory shelling and machine-gun fire. An enemy long distance gun dropped three shells into camp at rear H.Q. New C.O. arrived. CAPT. J.T. SCRIVEN.	
do.	19.12.17		CAPT. SCRIVEN took over command of the company from Lt. H.J. GOLDSPINK. H.Q. constituted at SIGNAL FARM. 4 more guns teams brought up to the	

WAR DIARY
or
INTELLIGENCE SUMMARY.

Army Form C. 2118.

Place	Date	Hour	Summary of Events and Information	Remarks and references to Appendices
REENINGHELST	20.12.17		anti-aircraft & recent duties at SIGNAL FARM. A quiet day on the line with the exception of shelling in FAIDHERBE X ROADS. Aircraft on both sides moderately active.	
			LT. H.T. GOLDSPINK left the company to proceed to M.S.C. Base Depot and was struck off strength. On the line everything was quiet except for occasional bursts of machine-gun fire along made from CINQ CHEMINS to the railway and to FAIDHERBE X ROADS. There was no ground activity. A heavy mist throughout the day made visibility very poor. Both sides sent up flares during the night. Both areas were shelled with gas-shells in large quantities especially the BROENBEER and STEEN BEEK valleys. The gas was intend to get forward to BOESINGHE.	
do.	21.12.17		There was again little activity on either side. The day being misty the kind spell of frost continued making going very difficult along the trench - tramo.	
do.	22.12.17		During the day enemy artillery and the trench tram worked. The troots were shelled and 5 CHEMINS and the nearest came in for special attention. A low flying plane was over at dawn apparently spotting for enemy artillery. Their trench-mortars were active on the right battalion area. Several times during the day enemy aircraft flew low over our lines and was fired on by our machine guns without success. About 4.15 p.m. a hostile raid took place on the TURENNE CROSSING posts. A heavy barrage was put down which was quickly replied to by all our artillery. In that our machine-guns on the right - both fired 3,500 rds. on S.O.S. lines and our trench-mortars were also active. Our machine-gun at the RAILWAY CROSSING was badly damaged by a shell and 3 O.R's were wounded. Lewis gun at SIGNAL POST was practically in the fire-line during the raid which finished about 5.30 pm. The enemy fire was observed to within 300 y's SNAG gun	

Army Form C. 2118.

WAR DIARY
or
INTELLIGENCE SUMMARY.
(Erase heading not required.)

Instructions regarding War Diaries and Intelligence Summaries are contained in F.S. Regs., Part II. and the Staff Manual respectively. Title pages will be prepared in manuscript.

Place	Date	Hour	Summary of Events and Information	Remarks and references to Appendices
KOEKUIT	23.12.17		Our artillery was very active during the day. Shelling posts captured by the enemy. Enemy artillery active on our day previous. During the night enemy rifle grenade and trench mortar batteries with gas shell. Signal post shell post-Norval	
do	24.12.17		A thaw set in and weather conditions improved. Visibility poor. During the afternoon our 4 guns at SIGNAL FARM were relieved by 2 guns & 143 M.G. Coy. During the afternoon our new position in Corps Defence Line at U10d 10.10. Also by 2 guns & 143 M.G. Coy. the relief of the 4 guns in the front line area was carried out after which our whole unit finished by 4 pm. Coys of relief parties attached. New camp taken over in BOESINGHE area and has H.Q. Sect. up at Bgd O.G.	
MARGUERITE CAMP Bgd O.G. (Sh. 28 N.W.)	25.12.17		Day spent in cleaning up and Xmas celebrations	
	26.12.17		Cleaning of guns and gun kit.— Kit inspection —	
	27.12.17		Gun - cleaning, PT, F.M.O. Inspection. Ends of feet.	
	28.12.17		Preparations made for the impending move — Baths —	
	29.12.17		Marched with Brigade to PLAISTOW CAMP, PROVEN. F 9.a 2.g. Sht 27	
	30.12.17		Company marched with Brigade to Code Area Q 23 & 24 ½ Sht 27 No stragglers	
	31.12.17		Company continued march to Huyssche Billets Withereclouds Camps. B.13.6 & 8. Sht 36 N.W. No stragglers	

M.W. Dickenson 2/Lt
O.C. 17 M.G. Coy

8th (IRISH) BATTALION "THE KING'S" (LIVERPOOL REGT).

ADMINISTRATIVE INSTRUCTIONS ISSUED
WITH O.O. 65.

26.12.18.

1. Officers Valises, Mess Kits and Blankets will be dumped at Q.M. Stores at 0830 Hours. Blankets will be rolled in bundles of ten and labelled clearly.

2. Billets will be left in a clean and sanitary condition. Lieut. H. Cheshire, M.C. will hand over Billets and obtain clean certificate from the Town Major.

3. Cookers and Lewis Gun Limbers will be ready for T.O. by 0930 Hours.

4. The unexpended portion of the days rations will be carried on Cookers.

5. Valises and Blankets etc will be drawn from Q.M. Stores on arrival at BERNEVILLE.

2/Lieut & Actg., Adjt.,
8th (Irish) Battn. K.L.Regt.

Issued at 1800 Hrs.
To all recipients of OO. 65.

From O.C
   171 M.G.Coy
To H.Q
   57 Div

Herewith the War Diary of 171 Machine Gun Company for the month of January

V. H. Wells Capt
  for O.C
  171 M.G.Coy

WAR DIARY
or
INTELLIGENCE SUMMARY.
(Erase heading not required.)

Army Form C. 2118.

171 M.G. Coy
Jan 1/18

Place	Date	Hour	Summary of Events and Information	Remarks and references to Appendices
ARMENTIERES	1.1.18		The company relieved the 9th Australian M.G.Coy in the ARMENTIERES Sector in the line. 6/7 H.A. established at B.30.c.30.05 and transport lines at B.23.b.00.20 (Sheet 36N.W.) Lifting positions taken out on the line. Fire guns during stopping fire from the support line and ten guns for main defence in the Subsidiary line. The sixteenth gun kept at Bn.Hd. in reserve and during A.A. work. Enemy artillery fire very inactive. Enemy machine-guns traversed and distributed fire during the night. We carried out indirect fire from J.14.a.11.02 on CROSS ROADS - NEZ MAQUART J.22.b.93.76. J.11.d.80.65 - 90.41, J.12.a.22.75, J.12.a.62.97. The following targets and also engaged J.11.d.80.65 - 90.41, J.12.a.22.75, J.12.a.62.97. J.14.b.68.37 - J.14.a.22.09. Total expenditure of S.A.A. 5000 rds.	
do.	2.1.18		Another very quiet day. Visibility very poor. Artillery on both sides extremely inactive. One of our planes flew over the Subsidiary line at 11.30 a.m. but was driven off by A.A. fire. Indirect machine gun fire was carried out on the following targets. CENSUS DRIVE C.24.c.7.5 - C.30.a.blue, IVANS TRENCH J.5.d.6.8 - J.5.d.4.3 CELT TRENCH C.14.d.05.05 - C.23.b.15.40. CENSOR DRIVE C.23.a.8.6 - C.24.c.40.58, CENTRAL TRENCH C.29.d.0.5 - J.5.d.5.9, CROSS ROADS - NEZ MAQUART J.22.b.93.76, PTE-RUELLE DE LA BLANCHE I.71.b.31.52, TRAMLINE J.5.a.22.20 - J.11.b.32.95, ROAD, RAILWAY BUILDINGS J.12.a.26.69.4 PTE. DE LA HONGRIE I.11.a.92.02. 10,000 rounds S.A.A. expended in all. Enemy machine-guns exceptionally quiet - indicative of a relief.	
do.	3.1.18		Owing to the high winds enemy artillery was very active especially in the HOUPLINES Sub-Sector on our right sector. A good deal of counter battery work took place on both sides. Enemy aircraft also active apparently taking photographs. Enemy machine-guns apparently grouped in batteries fired very ???	

Army Form C. 2118.

WAR DIARY
or
INTELLIGENCE SUMMARY.
(Erase heading not required.)

Instructions regarding War Diaries and Intelligence Summaries are contained in F. S. Regs., Part II. and the Staff Manual respectively. Title pages will be prepared in manuscript.

Place	Date	Hour	Summary of Events and Information	Remarks and references to Appendices
ARMENTIERES	3.1.18		Turned out my arms of day, turned out infantry & ranged their new artillery of aircraft, considerably active. Our machine gun fired 100 rnds of harassing aircraft during the day and at various intervals out the night. Approximate rounds fired on enemy — SAA 875 — 10,000 rounds being expended.	
do	4.1.18		During the day enemy artillery quiet, not so the mortars, 150 5.9 shells were counted falling onto BRULOTERIE during the night. British aeroplanes very active. Hostile planes also took place and one of the enemy machines appeared to be damaged, fell near one of our troops. Our Lewis gun Section were well placed and our M.G.s the enemy appeared flying close by. They sent no enemy machine guns activity during the night and M.G. officer's the Hussars, fire carried out round harassing fire on enemy tracks, and trenches in rear of enemy lines. S.A.A. rounds expended.	
do	5.1.18		Visibility was again poor and enemy & our own aircraft artillery was very in and indicators on the right side. We had no indication of any attack either. At 10.15 am a German Minister at 30 44mm. m. not took fire and a few mortars from the enemy. Harried - gun activity was very slight on the part of the enemy, the barrage at Saturday's place at intervals during the night. We carried out harassing fire to the extent of 8000 rds on enemy and enemy's fires.	

Army Form C. 2118.

WAR DIARY
or
INTELLIGENCE SUMMARY.
(Erase heading not required.)

Instructions regarding War Diaries and Intelligence Summaries are contained in F. S. Regs., Part II. and the Staff Manual respectively. Title pages will be prepared in manuscript.

Place	Date	Hour	Summary of Events and Information	Remarks and references to Appendices
ARMENTIERES	6.1.18		On the whole quiet day. ARMENTIERES was shelled at intervals during the day and the whole went the line also received attention. Subsidiary line was shelled with occasional 5·9 shells during the night. Enemy showed guns normal except one machine-gun fire behind ZERO. Friendly aircraft during the day and seven aeroplanes.	
do.	7.1.18		Left Sub-sector quiet. During the morning the enemy was busy on the support line. At night Our sector & enemy front worked to infantry-positions. Enemy shelled patrol. Two men and two during the morning. Our own aircraft are showing them are our lines. Our machine guns fired from the enemy the night on selected spots behind enemy line.	
do.	8.1.18		Enemy artillery and aircraft inactive and not non enterprising. Our trench mortars shot during the morning & shelled selected enemy machine-guns normal. Our own fired good at harassing fire by night.	
do.	9.1.18		The only attention our trench system received was a few rounds dropped into and near F.L. between 1 pm & 3 pm. Enemy artillery was engaged in harassing fire. Our 6" and heavy artillery retaliated on enemy artillery & positions. Two of our batteries patrolled around during the morning beyond their M.A. line. Enemy aircraft did not put in an appearance despite the clear visibility. A shortage started during the afternoon. Our machine guns fired 15000 rds in enemy rear, enemy machine-guns rare active.	
do.	10.1.18		Enemy artillery fact more active. Sharing signs of registration the vicinity of CAMBRIDGE AVENUE & IRISH AVENUE gun position etc. B22.8.9 also heavily shelled at noon. A large working party was working on Cafe farm FUSILIER AVE & TRESH AVE. The places were lit up at intervals. Half the firm went both our Mallard. Our own guns fired 15000 rds in selected targets by night.	

WAR DIARY or INTELLIGENCE SUMMARY

Army Form C. 2118.

Place	Date	Hour	Summary of Events and Information	Remarks and references to Appendices
ARMENTIERES	11.1.18		Enemy artillery on the whole quiet. 20 H.E. dropped in the vicinity of WESSEX AVE & GLOUCESTER AVE about 11am to which our artillery replied. In the night SHOWS, OLD DISTILLERY and the BRICKSTACK received a fair attention. Hostile trench mortars a bit active. — Enemy trench mortars active on the TIFFLES at nt. Enemy T.M.s fired upon also active of WILD STREETS and a pair to our patrolling prevented. Due to the moonlight. — Enemy machine gun normal. Day machine gun fire 11110 also harassing fire by night at the following new targets very engaged ENEMY M.G. C30 d 48 28, S-GIFTED Rd. I 60 b 82 — I 62 d 70 and DUMPS at C12C 30 2S & I 6 a 55 & 55. Trench mortars was put in at I 3b and I 1 c and position and ground latter slabs constructed.	
do.	12.1.18		Enemy artillery more active. Shelling our front system at intervals during the day. Our right sect. CHAPELLE ARMENTIERES received active attention during the day and the man's [?] up a bit. One of the Company's Lewis gun mounted in the wt. up the [?] being the Nightingale. Enemy trench mortars persistently shelled our front support lines. Aerial activity normal but machine-gun control not harassing fire by night on enemy dumps and e.t.s. & the delint. 11110.145	
do.	13.1.18		Day quiet. M2 HSCP relieved as on the line Relly complete without incident by Sections to little 5 head STEENWERCK 4.30 pm. Company proceeded by Sections to little's head STEENWERCK 65/148 established at Le GRAND BEAUMART, A.11 a.2.8	
STEENWERCK	14.1.18		Day spent in cleaning of guns & men	
	15.1.18		Further cleaning up. Special attention given to mens feet	
	16.1.18		A party of seventy men were sent on working parties mending communication in back areas in ARMENTIERES	

Army Form C. 2118.

WAR DIARY
or
INTELLIGENCE SUMMARY.
(Erase heading not required.)

Instructions regarding War Diaries and Intelligence
Summaries are contained in F.S. Regs., Part II.
and the Staff Manual respectively. Title pages
will be prepared in manuscript.

Place	Date	Hour	Summary of Events and Information	Remarks and references to Appendices
STEENWERCK	17.1.18		A party of six present are working parties. ARMENTIERES. Capt. SCRIVEN court-martialled held at STEENWERCK	
do	18/1/18		Two lorries cleaned & further cleaning up.	
do	19/1/18		Training, proper armament, gun cleaning, lectures etc.	
do	20/1/18		Sunday. - Church parade. further cleaning up.	
ARMENTIERES	21.1.18		The Company relieved 172 M.G. Coy. in the ARMENTIERES SECTOR of the Line. Relief completed by 5pm without incident. The day H.Q. & Transport Lines were taken over at B30c 30.65. and B23c 00.20 (sheet 26N.W.) Enemy artillery was active firing on CAMBRIDGE AVE & TISSAGE RD. The enemy Machine Guns were active during the night firing on C.T.S. - Aerial activity NIL - Trench Mortars heavy, ranged on our Front Line. Our Machine Guns fired 15,000 rounds - CROSS Roads I.22b.80.52, INCENSE CT. I.14.38.6.2.- FME DU HONGRI, I.14.4.92	
do	22.1.18		During the day enemy artillery was active. Shovels were fired into the town & vicinity of IRISH AVE Enemys Trench Mortars fired on our Front line. Enemys aerial activity considerable. Many A.A. & machine gun barrage put up on approach of our machines. - Enemys machine guns quiet by day. Our machine guns carried out most harassing fire on roads, tracks & in rear of enemys lines. 10,000 rounds expended.	
do	23.1.18.		Enemys artillery much quieter owing to low visibility. Enemy Trench Mortars fired on our Front Line & C.T.s. - Enemys Machine Guns less active during the day & night. Enemys Aircraft - Normal. Our Artillery was more active than usual firing on truck areas. Our machine guns fired 10,000 rounds on enemy's back areas. 10 R wounded by shell fire. ROAD = 6a.15/65 LE TEMPLE C.30d.9.0. TRACK I.11d.40.95-I.11c.80.95.	
do	24.1.18.		During the day the enemy artillery was normal. Enemys Machine guns were again noticeably active by day against our aircraft. Enemys Trench Mortars quiet. Shelling the Mays. Our Machine guns fired on ROAD = 6a.15/65 LE TEMPLE C.30d.9.0. TRACK I.11d.40.95-I.11c.80.95. 12,000 rounds expended.	

Army Form C. 2118.

WAR DIARY
or
INTELLIGENCE SUMMARY.
(Erase heading not required.)

Instructions regarding War Diaries and Intelligence Summaries are contained in F. S. Regs., Part II. and the Staff Manual respectively. Title pages will be prepared in manuscript.

Place	Date	Hour	Summary of Events and Information	Remarks and references to Appendices
ARMENTIERES	25.1.18		Enemy artillery quiet on the Right sub Sector, on the Left Sub Sector his artillery was active firing on O.T.s & Support line. Hostile Aircraft were more active, several planes flying low along our Front line & Support line during the day. Enemy Machine guns were very active during the night. Our Machine guns carried out road harassing fire on roads, Tracks &c Ta Ca Farm huts in rear of enemy's lines. 12,800 rounds expended. 10 R wounded by machine gun bullet.	
do	26.1.18		During the day enemy artillery quiet owing to low visibility. A few H.E. shells fired on Spam Avenue. Hostile aircraft Nil. Enemy Trench active on our Front Line. The silence on enemy machine guns during the night was noticeable. Our machine fired on BATH.H.Q. at I.19.b.92.5.8 & on roads, O.Ts &c during the night. 12,200 rounds expended.	
do	27.1.18		Day Quiet. 172 M.G. Coy relieved us in the line. Relief completed without incident by 4.30 pm. One Section was left under the charge of 173 M.G. Coy for the defence of ARMENTIERES. The Company proceeded by sections to its old billets near STEENWERCK. Coy H Q established at LE GRAND BEAUMART.	
STEENWERCK	28.1.18		Day spent in cleaning up of men and guns.	
do	29.1.18		The Company rested. Remainder of the day spent on repacking limbers.	
do	30.1.18		Training program commenced. Lectures & Arms Drill.	
do	31.1.18		The Company went by motor lorry to ARMENTIERES to take part in a barrage for a raid by 172 Inf Bde. The Company returned by motor lorry arriving in billets 3.30 am the raid having been cancelled. Captain [illegible] The Medicine on Captain SCRIVEN (summoned the service) was unsuccessful.	

W.A. Wells Capt for O.C.
171 M.G. Coy

WAR DIARY
or
INTELLIGENCE SUMMARY.
(Erase heading not required.)

Army Form C. 2118.

Place	Date	Hour	Summary of Events and Information	Remarks and references to Appendices
STEENWERCK	1.2.18		The Company went by motor buses to ARMENTIERES to take part in the M.G. Barrage for the raid by 172 Inf Bde. Zero hour 7.30 p.m. The raid was successful & prisoners being obtained. 49,000 rounds were expended.	
ARMENTIERES	2.2.18		The Company relieved 172 M.G. Coy in the ARMENTIERES Sector. The relief completed without incident by 4.30 pm. The enemy artillery showed little activity in spite of good observation. Enemy Machine Guns were very active all day against our aircraft by night the firing was slightly below normal. During the night considerable number of aeroplanes were up. Our Machine guns fired 8,000 rounds of ammunition on roads etc	
do	3.2.18		The last day past without anything of importance. The enemy Machine guns were again active rifling our aircraft. Our Machine guns fired on the usual Targets 10,000 rounds being expended.	
do	4.2.18		Situation normal expect for very heavy hostile Machine Gun fire on our aircraft. Our machine guns fired on roads, tramways etc 9,800 rounds of S.A.A. being expended.	
do	5.2.18		Enemy Artillery fairly active on its counter battery work. Hostile heavy Machine Gun fire on our aircraft. Our aircraft was hotly engaged by the enemy A.A. guns immediately they came into range. Our machine guns fired on the usual targets 6,000 rounds of S.A.A. being expended. 8 guns in the L'EPINETTE sector were relieved by 8 guns of 172 Machine gun Company. The relieved sections took up position in the ARMENTIERES Defences. The relief was completed by 1 p.m. The Company billets were moved into RUE D'ERQUINGHEM.	
do	6.2.18		Situation normal during the afternoon & evening. A raid was carried out by the 2/4 K.L.R. at 8.30pm. Our Machine Guns carried out a barrage in support on the enemys front line & left-guns being used. Total expenditure during the barrage was 22,500 rounds. 10 prisoners were taken.	
do	7.2.18		The day past without any event. The Enemy Machine Guns were unusually quiet during the night. Our Machine Guns fired on Roads in the enemy back areas expending 3,000 rounds of S.A.A.	

Army Form C. 2118.

WAR DIARY
or
INTELLIGENCE SUMMARY.
(Erase heading not required.)

Instructions regarding War Diaries and Intelligence Summaries are contained in F.S. Regs., Part II. and the Staff Manual respectively. Title pages will be prepared in manuscript.

Place	Date	Hour	Summary of Events and Information	Remarks and references to Appendices
ARMENTIERES	8.2.18		The enemy artillery was quiet during the day & night. The enemy machine guns was very active just after dusk and they were unusually quiet during the remainder of the night. Our Machine guns fired on C.T.s JUNC TRAM WAY D25A 1075. CENTRAL AVENUE C29A 90.55.15 C300 95.35. TRAMLINE I6A 15.55. 10,000 rounds of S.A.A. being expended. LIEUT W.F.A. BLACKMAN proceeded on leave.	
do	9.2.18		The enemys artillery was normal. The enemy Machine guns were very active throughout the night. Own machine guns carried out the normal overnight fire on enemy back areas 40,000 rounds being expended.	
do	10.2.18		The enemy artillery was on the whole more active & appeared to be registering on F.L. C.T.s & S.L. a certain amount of neutrons shelling took place during the night. Own machine guns fired on the normal target for the evening. Back areas 40,000 rounds of S.A.A. being expended.	
do	11.2.18		Nothing unusual to report. a quiet day Own Machine guns carried out the usual indirect fire 16,500 rounds of S.A.A. being expended	
do	12.2.18		Nothing unusual to report. Own machine guns carried out the normal indirect fire 15,000 rounds of S.A.A being expended. The advance party of 114 Machine gun Company arrived.	
do	13.2.18		The Company was relieved by 114 Machine gun Company in daylight. The relief completed by 3pm. The Company proceeded to hutted at L2362.7. CAPT R.A.T MILLER reported to O.C. Company.	
ESTAIRES	14.2.18		Day spent in cleaning up. Particular attention was paid to cleaning up of guns Kilts.	
do	15.2.18		Further cleaning up. Limbers cleaned & painted, guns & parts cleaned.	
do	16.2.18		Training for the Company. Gun Drill, & Arms Drill foot inspection etc	
do	17.2.18		Being Sunday "No Training". Kit inspection	
do	18.2.18 19.2.18 20.2.18 21.2.18 22.2.18 23.2.18		Training continued no 57 Machine gun Battalion Orders	

Army Form C. 2118.

WAR DIARY
or
INTELLIGENCE SUMMARY.

(Erase heading not required.)

Instructions regarding War Diaries and Intelligence Summaries are contained in F. S. Regs., Part II. and the Staff Manual respectively. Title pages will be prepared in manuscript.

Place	Date	Hour	Summary of Events and Information	Remarks and references to Appendices
ESTAIRES	24.2.18		Day being Sunday no training. Kit inspection.	AM
"	25.2.18		Training continued as per Battn Orders. Arms Drill:- T.O.E.T. practised with the recruits in: Musketry. - Short practice on miniature range. The afternoon were devoted to recreational training (rugby shoes foot ball matches etc)	
"	26.2.18			
"	27.2.18			

B.H. Miller Capt.
OC
171 Coy M.G.C.